SCALING

THE STEPS

OF

SUCCESS...

Birister Sharma

Copyright © 2022 Birister Sharma

All Rights Reserved.

Made with ❤on the Notion Press Platform

www.notionpress.com

Dedicated to my loving wife....

Pallabi Devi Sharma

I surrendered to you, O my Lord……

"Om Namah Shivaya"

Table of Contents

One Word

Do you have a principle in your life? If not, then make a principle in your life. It is a must-have for you. A man without principles never achieves anything in his life. What is the principle of your life? Your principle of life is to live the best life, no matter what happens. Your principle of life is to become a winner. Your principle of life is to become a successful person. Your principle of life is to live a dignified life.

You're born with natural talents and abilities. But if you have no principle of life, then your natural talents and abilities are worthless. You can't do anything. It is only your principle of life that awakens your dormant potential. You have infinite energy and power within you. You have to awaken it. You have to ignite it.

Have you ever asked yourself why you are in this world? No. You're in this world to make a difference not only in your life but also in your dear ones' lives. You have every right to make your life beautiful. You have every reason to make your life meaningful.

Always remember that a man without principles is directionless. He is like a bird without wings. He is like a ship without an anchor. He is like a blind person. He is like a mute. He is like a lame person. He will always wander throughout his entire life.

What do you want in your life? A happy life or an unhappy life? The choice is yours.

A man of principle is always clear in his visions and directions. He knows his mission in life. He will always move ahead in his life. He will stand tall and firm like a giant mountain at every juncture of his life.

Always try to become a man of principle. Only your principles in life will lead you to the path of happiness and success.

Your principle of life is to live with dignity.

Your principle of life is to be happy.

Your principle of life is to be graceful.

Your principle of life is to be positive.

Your principle of life is to be motivated.

Your principle of life is to be energetic.

Your principle of life is to be enthusiastic.

Your principle of life is to be powerful.

Your principle of life is to be brave.

Your principle of life is to be successful.

---***---

1. Be responsible

If you want grand success in your life, then the only mantra for your success lies within you. There is no other external source remaining for you. It's only you. It's only you. You're the only one responsible for your success. You're the only one responsible for your failure.

You're responsible for everything you think or do in your life. You're responsible for everything you plan or decide in your life. Never blame anybody if you ever fail to execute your thoughts, plans, decisions, and actions, because you're solely responsible for everything. You're responsible for every outcome in your life.

If you're successful in your life, then you're the only one responsible for your success.

If you fail in your life, then you're the only one responsible for your failure.

You will never share your success or failure with anybody in your life.

Your life is like a small seed of a plant; the way you sow it is the way you reap its fruits. But you have to toil for it, both day in and day out, day and night. Only then will you get what you want from it. Your success always depends on you. It is in your hands. You can make it the way you want, and you can shape it the way you wish.

If you have a good amount of money in your pocket, then it depends on you whether you spend it for a good cause or for a bad cause. You're responsible for either cause.

You're like the goldsmith of your life. You can convert your life into any form or design of jewels.

You've an infinite source of talents and skills hidden within yourself. It is your responsibility to unearth them yourself. You've to realize your potential. Nobody will come to you to awaken your quiescent potentials. It is only you who will have to awaken them. Only then can you mold and nurture your talents and skills into your grand success.

It is always up to you what you want in your life: success or failure; happiness or unhappiness.

Let us suppose that if a living room is completely shut in the shadows of darkness, then it is up to you whether you would switch on the lights and brighten your living room, or you would keep your living room in complete darkness as before. Many people desperately want to achieve great success in their lives, but their problem is that they never want to switch on their lives. They like to live their lives in darkness.

They are always waiting for great things to happen in their lives. They are waiting for great opportunities rather than working hard on their abilities. Waiting for great opportunities is not a bad thing, but doing nothing is a bad thing for you. You'll get nothing. You'll always remain empty-handed.

Always remember that it is only your hard work that knocks at the doors of great opportunities.

Try to create your own opportunities in your life with your own responsibilities.

There are many great men who have created great histories while creating their own opportunities in their lives, like Dhirubhai Ambani, Henry Ford, Bill Gates, Mark Zuckerberg, and many more. They never waited for great opportunities to happen in their lives.

They have made things happen in their lives. They have created their own opportunities.

Is there anything that happens by itself without doing anything?

If anybody thinks so, then it is a foolish act. He will never gain anything in his life. He will never reach anywhere. He will only revolve like a spinning top.

But there are many people who think like this. And they, knowingly and unknowingly, repeat it over and over again. They never learn anything from their mistakes in their entire lives. And they are always blaming others, living a mediocre life.

If you want to relish the scrumptious dish today, then what will you do first in your kitchen? Obviously, you would buy the best ingredients for your dish. Then you start preparing it according to the requirements, such as cutting, peeling, and washing. When everything is ready, you start cooking your dish and allow it some time to cook. After some time, you'll get the wafting sweet and delicious smell of your dish all around your kitchen as well as in your living room. Finally, you'll relish your favorite dish with your heart's content.

Similarly, if you want to relish the scrumptious success in your life, then everything relies on you. You've got to think. You've got to plan. You've got to decide. You've got to prepare. And finally, you've got to act. Nobody will come to help you. You've got to help yourself. You're responsible for everything.

Nobody will become a better cook than you in your life because you know what the best ingredients for your life are.

This life is yours, as is your success or failure. You're responsible for everything. Everything is on your shoulders, whether you accept it or reject it; whether you mend it or break it. You've got to think for yourself. You've got to plan for yourself. You've got to decide for yourself. You've got to prepare for yourself. And you've got to execute for yourself.

But first of all, you must know your strong points and your weak points before you act on any of your commitments. Because when you know your strengths and weaknesses, only then can you easily execute them in the best possible manner.

You must know what is good for you and what is bad for you; after all, you're responsible for your own life. One good decision may lead you to the sparkling brightness of success, while one bad decision may lead you to the engulfing darkness of failure.

You're like the scriptwriter of your own film. You can write any story you like in your script. You're responsible for your own story. Whether your story is a hit or a flop, you're solely responsible. You should never blame anybody for your success or failure.

If you get a blank piece of paper, then it is up to you what you want to write on it. If you want to write "success" on it, then you can write it. And if you want to write "failure" on it, then you can write that as well. The choice is always yours.

You're responsible for yourself, whatever you think; whatever you plan; whatever you decide; whatever you prepare; and whatever you act.

Your life is like a white paper. Whether you write something on it, or you leave it blank, or you tear it. Whether you write success on it, or you write failure on it. Everything depends upon you. You've to think for yourself. You've to plan for yourself. You've to decide for yourself. You've to prepare for yourself. You've to act for yourself. After all, you're solely responsible for your own life.

You're the sole responsible for your success.

You're the sole responsible for your failure.

Think and Act

You are responsible for your life. You can't keep blaming somebody else for your dysfunction. Life is really about moving on.

---Orpah Winfreg

You are the one who is responsible for your failure.....You are the one who is responsible for your success. At any cost don't blame others.

Challenges make you more responsible. Always remember that life without struggle is a life without success. Don't give up and learn not to quit.

Each man is questioned by life; and he can only answer to life by answering for his own life; to life he can only respond by being responsible.

---Viktor Frankl

You cannot escape the responsibility of tomorrow by evading it today.

---Abraham Lincoln

---***---

2. Reinvent yourself

Reinvent means transforming yourself from good to better, and from better to best.

Reinvent means turning yourself into perfection.

Reinvent means making yourself into excellence.

Reinvent means finding your hidden potential.

Reinvent means knowing your true self.

Everything already exists in this world. For instance, all five elements of our life—air; water, fire, earth, and sky—already exist in this world. We just need to reinvent them for ourselves, which means modifying them for our requirements.

When a scientist works in his laboratory in order to invent something new, he devotes himself entirely to his experiment. He totally forgets himself and everything around him. He is only aware of his experiment. He works throughout the day and night, skipping his lunch, rest, and sleep, concentrating on one single-minded goal. He works like a madman. He forgets about his health and his family. He forgets all his attachments and commitments to worldly affairs until he succeeds in his experiment. Finally, after many days, many weeks, many months, and many years of hard, tiring experiments, he comes out of his lab with flying colors and proclaims his invention to the world.

This world is like your lab, and you're like a scientist of your life. You've got to devote yourself completely to inventing new things for yourself. You've got to work hard with one single-minded goal, day in and day out, to create something special for yourself. No doubt, there are many hurdles coming your way every second, every minute, every hour, every day, every week, every month, and every year, waiting for you with their opening jaws to trap you. But you've got to work hard like a madman, forgetting everything. Only then will you glimpse the bright sunshine of your success.

When you reinvent yourself, you'll know your energy.

When you reinvent yourself, you'll know your power.

When you reinvent yourself, you'll know your strength.

When you reinvent yourself, you'll know your skills.

When you reinvent yourself, you'll know your talents.

When you reinvent yourself, you'll know your weaknesses.

When you reinvent yourself, you'll know your positive points.

When you reinvent yourself, you'll know your negative points.

When you reinvent yourself, you'll know the goals of your life.

When you reinvent yourself, you'll find the directions of your life.

When you reinvent yourself, you'll unearth the hidden treasures of your life.

When a weightlifter lifts any weight for the first time in his life, he only lifts a weight half of his body weight. Then, later on, as he starts practicing more and more and lifting more and more weights, he realizes that he can lift more weights than his actual body weight.

What does it show?

It shows that the weightlifter already has the potential to lift more weights than his real body weight.

In a similar way, you have the potential for everything within you; you just need to realize it and reinvent yourself.

You have to reinvent yourself to achieve your grand success.

Always remember that nobody will care about you if you fail in your life.

If you fail in your life, it means you're like an orphan child in this world. Nobody will come to you. You have nobody in this world. You have to live your life alone. You have no friends. Everybody will ignore you, disregard you, and treat you like a villain.

On the contrary, if you're successful in your life, then everybody will flock around you. You'll never feel alone. You've thousands of friends. Everybody will care about you, respect you, and treat you like a hero.

You couldn't achieve grand success in your life until and unless you reinvent yourself. This world is changing very fast. Now and then, you'll find new changes, new transformations, and new challenges. You can't stop anything. What was yesterday wouldn't be the same today, nor would it be similar in the successive days, nor would it be identical in the following months, nor would it be equal in the coming years.

Everything is changing now and then, every time, every moment, and every day. So you've to change yourself and reinvent yourself according to time and need in order to find your best place in this world.

Many people fail in their lives not because they lack skills and talents; it is because they fail to reinvent their hidden potential at the right time. It is like a treasure house that lies within them, and unfortunately, they do not know themselves.

Once upon a time, in a small village, there lived a beggar. He had spent his entire life begging door to door in the houses of villagers. He had no place to live, so he stayed under the banyan tree on the outskirts of the village. Many years elapsed in the same way. He became very old, and then one day he passed away. The village folks cremated his dead body and performed all the rituals.

Then one day, the village folks cut down the banyan tree and dug out the place where the beggar used to stay. When the village folks dug out the place, they were stunned; what they saw was a huge casket of gold coins. With that much treasure, the beggar would have been the richest man in the entire village and in the entire area. But, alas, the poor beggar had spent his entire life begging door to door in the houses of villagers.

You'll become like a beggar if you fail to reinvent yourself. You'll always wander through your entire life without knowing your actual potential. You have a tremendous treasure house within you. You have to reinvent it yourself.

Reinvent yourself if you want to uncover your treasure house.

Reinvent your hidden treasure house of skills and talents, because if you can't reinvent yourself, then you'll never compete in this highly competitive world. You'll never cope with the changing things, situations, or problems in your everyday life.

When you reinvent yourself, only then will you know the definite goals of your life; only then will you know the purpose of your life; only then will you know the missions of your life; only then will you fulfill your dreams and turn them into realities; only then will you achieve great success in your life.

When you reinvent yourself, you'll know what you have to do in your life. You'll know how to live in this world. You'll know the directions of your life. You'll know how to achieve success in your life.

You can only develop yourself when you know your hidden treasures of skills and talents.

Whenever you feel morally down, this is the right time to reinvent yourself.

Whenever you feel weak, this is the right time to reinvent yourself.

Whenever you feel you are losing your self-confidence, this is the right time to reinvent yourself.

Whenever you feel confused, this is the right time to reinvent yourself.

Whenever you feel you are wandering from the path of your life, this is the right time to reinvent yourself.

When you reinvent yourself, only then will you know the infinite hidden skills and talents within you.

Your hidden skills and talents are the best boons of your life. You have every right to know these hidden treasures. And once you know your hidden treasures, you'll become the most valuable gem in this world. Then nothing is impossible for you. Everything is possible for you. Everything is achievable for you.

The gold mine is always hidden deep inside the earth. Nobody can ever see it from above until it is dug out.

In the same way, you too have a gold mine deep inside you; until you dig it out, you won't know how valuable you are. And once you do this, you'll realize how much treasure is lying within you.

To get any success in your life, first of all, you've to dig out your hidden skills and talents, and then work on them with full determination and zest. Then you'll get whatever you want in your life. Your success will become your servant, and you'll become its master.

But every time, every moment, and every day you've to reinvent your hidden skills and talents, and then polish them and nurture them day in and day out.

Everything is within you.

You have a tremendous treasure house lying within you.

You can do anything in your life.

Nothing is impossible for you.

You can achieve any success in your life.

You can touch any summit in your life.

Nobody can stop you.

But you have to know your hidden potential.

You have to reinvent yourself.

Once you know your hidden skills and talents, then nobody will ever dare to stop you from reaching your goal.

You will become the master of your destiny.

You will become the sole maker of your fortune.

Reinvent yourself.

Reinvent your life.

Reinvent your world.

You've to reinvent your skills and talents every time, every moment and every day. Then only you'll get grand success in your life.

Think and Act

Every day is a chance to reinvent yourself and become brand new.

You are never too old to reinvent yourself.

---Steve Harvey

Life isn't about finding yourself. Life is about creating yourself.

---George Bernard Shaw

When things are bad, it's the best time to reinvent yourself.

---George Lopez

T.......Time to

R.......Reinvent

Y.......Yourself

---***---

3. No action, no progress

We all know Newton's third law: For every action, there is an equal and opposite reaction. The statement means that in every interaction, there is a pair of forces acting on the two interacting objects. The size of the force on the first object equals the size of the force on the second object.

From Newton's third law, we can conclude that in our lives, without action, there is no progress. You must act to make progress in your life. When you act, only then will you achieve progress in your life, and only then will you achieve success in your life.

No action, no progress, and no success.

Action signifies your progress in life, and progress signifies your success in life. Whatever you do in your life will reflect on your life, transfer to your progress, and then convert into your success.

Inaction means degradation in your life. Degradation means you fail in your life. Ask yourself what you want in your life: action or inaction, success or failure.

Without action, you can't think anything with your mind.

Without action, you can't see anything with your eyes.

Without action, you can't smell anything with your nose.

Without action, you can't taste anything with your tongue.

Without action, you can't chew anything with your teeth.

Without action, you can't speak anything with your mouth.

Without action, you can't work anything with your hands.

Without action, you can't walk anywhere with your legs.

These actions of your life are natural. These are the ongoing processes, never-ending. You can't stop these actions. However, the moment you try to pause these actions of your life is the moment you halt your own life.

Can you live your life without action?

You never live your life without action. You have to act on something in order to live your life. It is impossible to live your life without action. Your action is a part of your life. Your action is the root of your world where you're standing right now. You never depart from your action.

Right from the moment we are born into this world, our action starts and ends at the last moment when we take our last breath. So, action is a natural phenomenon and fundamental to our life. We never detach ourselves from our action. We are all uniformly connected with our actions. And that's why we are existing now.

Action is your life.

Without action, your life is impossible.

It is only your action that makes your life possible.

Your action gives you new movements in your life.

Your action gives you new ways in your life.

Your action gives you new purpose in your world.

Always remember that only your action guarantees you happiness, progress, success, and peace in your life. Only your action makes you a complete man in your life.

With your action, you're alive. Without action, you're dead.

A man becomes a complete man with his action.

Think for a second: if our Earth stops revolving around the sun, then what will happen? Everything will become imbalanced in the entire world, and our life will become impossible on Earth.

In the same fashion, the moment you stop your actions, your entire life and world become imbalanced and disturbed.

Action makes your life balanced. And when there is balance in your life, it means there is happiness and success in your world. However, inaction only creates imbalance and chaos in your life. And when there is imbalance and chaos in your life, it means there is unhappiness and failure in your world.

Can you live your life in imbalance?

No. You can never live your life in imbalance.

Whenever you fall ill, it signifies that some parts of your body are not functioning well or are not acting properly. So whenever you feel weak or sick, it always indicates that your body is not doing well or is in an inactive mood, and you need to take action or you need medicine.

This implies that you always need action in every moment of your life. Whenever there is a slight lack of your action, there is the beginning of your weakness and sickness.

A healthy life is the sight of action. A poor life is the sight of inaction.

Your life is like a vehicle. It will only run on the smooth road of your balanced life. You will never run it on the rough road of an imbalanced life.

Your life is like a motorbike. If you want to start it, then you'll have to kick it; that means you'll have to act on it. Only then will the motorbike of your life start zooming on the road of your progress, happiness, success, and peace.

Even without action, the king of the forest, the lion, couldn't hunt its prey. If a lion wants to hunt its prey, then it has to act. If it is simply sleeping and daydreaming of a stout deer as its prey, which will enter into its mouth itself, then it is total foolishness.

It is only through the action of a man that he can turn a mere stone into gold and a precious diamond.

Do you know how a pearl is formed inside the seashell from a small dew drop?

When a small dew drop is stuck inside the sea shell, with the tremendous internal actions and reactions inside the sea shell, the small dew drop transforms itself into a beautiful shining pearl after some days.

What does it exemplify to you? Think about it!

Does the miracle happen in life? Yes, miracles do happen in life. If you want to glimpse the miracles in your life, then you have to act every moment of your life.

You'll never get anything simply by building a magnificent castle in the air.

With your actions, you can do anything in your life.

You can change yourself.

You can transform yourself.

You can achieve anything in your life.

Action means energy.

Action means power.

Action means strength.

Inaction means sickness.

Inaction means weakness.

Inaction means idleness.

Where there is action, there is also reaction. On the other hand, where there is no action, there is no reaction. And when both action and reaction are absent in your life, then your life will turn into a void and become meaningless.

In stagnant water, you'll only find the aquatic life that lives either inside the mud or inside the holes, like frogs, crabs, worms, and snakes. You'll never see the freely swimming fish and other aquatic animals there. There are no actions and movements in stagnant water, and one day it'll dry up with the heat of the sun, killing all the aquatic life living there.

In the same way, you can't live your life in a stagnant state. You need actions and movements in your life so that you can swim in the ocean of this world, gather the seashells containing pearls, and reach the next shore of your life.

In every stage of your life, you need action to progress. Without action, you couldn't move even a plate of bread inside your mouth. Without action, you'll remain starving. Without action, your life is like a tree without leaves.

In plant life, the roots are the most important components. The survival of a plant depends on the actions of the roots because they are the carriers of water, minerals, and manure from the underground soil. If the roots stop their actions of carrying water, minerals, and manure from the underground soil, the plant will die instantly the moment the roots stop their actions.

In a similar way, your actions are the roots of your life, guiding you towards the road of progress and success. It is only your actions that hold you up every time you're about to tumble down in life. If you stop your actions the moment you witness the sight of doom, you will struggle. On the other hand, once you resume your actions, you'll see glimpses of your bright progress and grand success right away.

Do you know why some people achieve great progress and success in their lives while others achieve nothing in their entire lives?

The people who achieve great progress and success are truly hard-working individuals. They are people of action. Their lives are full of actions and excitement. They believe in their hard work and live through their actions.

On the other hand, the people who achieve nothing in their entire lives are lazy and inactive. They are the people of inaction. They are only daydreamers. Their lives are full of idleness and boredom. They believe in their luck and live in their dream worlds.

Where do you find yourself in these two categories of people?

Find out your answer.

Always remember that the way you act is the way you become in your life.

Action means your life.

Inaction means your death.

You can't live without action.

You have to act in order to live your life.

Your action is the only source of your happiness.

Your action is the only source of your progress.

Your action is the only source of your success.

Your action is the only source of your peace.

No action, no happiness.

No action, no progress.

No action, no success.

No action, no peace.

It is only your action that gives meaning to your life.

It is only your action that shows you the purpose of your life.

You're born to act, but not to remain idle.

Your action brings you happiness and prosperity in your life, while your inaction brings you unhappiness and adversity.

Every living creature on this earth takes some action in order to exist.

You exist in this world because you are taking action in your life.

Where there is action, there is progress and there is success in your life.

Where there is no action, there is no progress and there is no success.

Think and Act

You may never know what results come from your action. But if you do nothing, there will be no result.

---Mahatma Gandhi

Action is the foundational key to all success.

---Pablo Picasso

Don't talk, act. Don't say, show. Don't promise, prove.

The distance between your dreams and reality is called action.

The path to success is to take massive determined action.

---Tony Robbins

---***---

4. Persistence

Your life is like a race, and if you want to win this race of your life, then you've got to work hard with persistence. Without persistence in your work, you'll never succeed in anything. Without persistence, you just forget your wishes, forget your desires, forget your dreams, and forget your aims and objectives, because without persistence, you can't do anything in your life.

To achieve anything in your life, you need persistence. You need persistence in your thoughts. You need persistence in your ideas. You need persistence in your plans. You need persistence in your decisions. You need persistence in your actions. You need persistence in your work. You need persistence in whatever you do in your life. When you've got persistence in everything, then only will you achieve grand success in your life.

Persistence is the only key factor to achieve anything in your life.

Where there is no persistence, there is no work, and there is no success. Without persistence in your work, you can never expect anything. It is only your persistence that guarantees you grand success in your life. Persistence means:

PERSEVERANCE

DETERMINATION

DOGGEDNESS

DILIGENCE

RESOLUTION

Persistence is the combination of these five strong qualities. That means if you have persistence, then automatically all these five strong qualities (perseverance, determination, doggedness, diligence, and resolution) will emerge from you.

Persistence means to stick to your chosen goal until the end, until you get what you've desired or dreamed of.

Without persistence, you'll become weak and worthless. Without persistence, you'll never witness the bright sight of your victory. Without persistence, you'll never perceive the shining glory of your life.

Without persistence, nothing is possible.

Without persistence, your life is impossible.

Without persistence, you'll never fulfill your dreams into your reality.

Persistence means to work continuously until you get your desired result.

Persistence means never giving up.

It is only your persistence that makes you realize your hidden talents and skills.

One day, a man was told by a holy saint that there was a place at the mount of the hill where abundant gold treasures were hidden under the earth. But he had to dig a deep tunnel in order to unearth the gold treasures from there.

The man was overwhelmed with joy. He instantly got ready, went to the mount of the hill, and started digging day and night, tirelessly. Many days and months passed; he had dug a long tunnel at the mount of the hill, but unfortunately, he couldn't get a glimpse of any gold treasure inside.

The man was dejected. He thought that he had been fooled by a holy saint. He lost his hope and confidence. He was out of patience, and finally, he gave up his persistence.

Then, one day, a shepherd came inside the tunnel coincidentally while tending to his herd of sheep at the foot of the hill. He went inside the deep tunnel, strolled there, and reached the end of the tunnel. When he reached the end of the tunnel, he glimpsed a sight of a glittering stone. He was overjoyed. He immediately dug out the rest of the tunnel and found abundant gold treasures.

Likewise, in the above story, there are many people who work hard with persistence, but due to a lack of self-belief, self-confidence, and patience, they give up their work when they are very close to reaching their gold treasures.

Whatever you do in your life, always remember that with your persistent work, you too need firm self-belief, self-confidence, and patience. Only then will you reach your final goal and become a successful person in your life.

With persistence, a weak man becomes a strong man.

With persistence, a strong man becomes stronger.

With persistence, an ordinary man becomes an extraordinary man.

With persistence, an imperfect man becomes a perfect man.

With persistence, you can become a master in your work.

With your persistence, you can unlock your closed fortune.

If you ever get lost on the way to success, then it is only your sheer persistence that guides you to move ahead.

You couldn't achieve anything in your life without persistence. But if you have the quality of persistence within you, then you have nothing to worry about, because you can achieve anything. Everything is possible for you. Your hands will become capable of doing anything for you. Your legs will become capable of moving you everywhere. You can easily grab whatever you want in your life with your two hands. You can easily move wherever you want to go with your two legs. You can cover every milestone of success in your life.

Think for a second: if our heart stops beating for a microsecond, what will happen to us? No doubt, within a microsecond we'll die from heart failure. But it is our heart that beats persistently and non-stop to keep us alive.

Think for a second: if the blood circulation in our body stops suddenly, what will happen to us? No doubt, within a few seconds we'll die from the choking of blood vessels. But our blood circulation is functioning persistently to keep us alive.

Think for a second: if our breathing nostrils stop abruptly, what will happen to us? No doubt, we'll die of suffocation within a few seconds. But our nostrils are breathing persistently to keep us alive.

Persistence is the natural order.

It is the fundamental law of our life.

Without it, nobody could live in this world.

Whatever you see around you—like cars, motors, houses, big buildings, electric goods and gadgets, computers, robots, airplanes, aircraft, rockets, and spaceships—all are the products of man's die-hard persistence.

Before the 18th century, it was impossible for a man to reach into space. It was quite impossible to think or imagine; it was beyond our reach. We had no idea what things exactly existed in space or outer space.

But our great scientists didn't give up. They were focused and stuck to their great experiments. They had persistently worked harder and harder, and then in the beginning of the 19th century, they invented rockets, space shuttles, and spaceships, and reached into space as well as outer space, discovering all the mysteries of space, finding solar systems, the Milky Way, and other celestial bodies of our universe.

These inventions and discoveries of rockets, space shuttles, spaceships, the solar system, the Milky Way, and celestial bodies by our great scientists imply that nothing is impossible in this world if we work persistently toward our chosen goals or missions with a single-minded focus.

Everything is possible with our persistence. With our continuous efforts and persistence, we can invent or discover anything in our lives. Nothing is beyond our reach. We can reach anywhere. We can decipher anything in this world.

Your persistence is the only source of energy to ignite your success.

If there is persistence, there is your success.

If there is no persistence, there is only your failure.

There is great power in your persistence.

Have you seen a stone cutter by the roadside, breaking a giant boulder with his small hammer?

If you ever see a stone cutter by the roadside, you'll always see a heap of broken pieces of stone beside him.

How could a stone cutter break a giant boulder into small pieces of stone with his small hammer? Could he break a giant boulder in just one stroke with his small hammer? No.

A stone cutter couldn't break a giant boulder into small pieces of stone with his first stroke. He has to strike again and again. Ten times. One hundred times. One thousand times. A countless number of times. He has to strike persistently over and over again. Then finally, it'll break with just one final stroke.

What does it signify to you?

It signifies that no matter how tough or how giant your situation or problem may be, you'll be able to overcome it with your sheer efforts and persistence.

Consider yourself a stone cutter, and strike again and again, tirelessly toward your chosen goals with single-minded determination, and then go ahead; your D-day will finally arrive.

If you see a flowing river over the deep gorges, then you would see how it cuts through the hard rocks and forms its way. It is only possible because of the persistent work of a river. A river is always flowing slowly, but it continuously cuts the hard surface of rocks with its sharp waves and currents, and gradually it creates its own path after many long days, weeks, months, and years. And finally, it reaches its ultimate destiny in the heart of the vast ocean.

Be like a river and carve your own path in the midst of hard rock-like situations and problems in your life. Believe in yourself. Believe in your capabilities. Work persistently until you reach your final destiny. You'll definitely achieve a hundred percent success in your life.

The Taj Mahal is one of the Seven Wonders of the World. Do you know how many years it took to complete the entire construction and how many laborers worked on it?

To complete the entire Taj Mahal, it took more than twenty years, and more than twenty thousand labourers worked. The labourers worked day and night, non-stop, tirelessly for more than twenty years until the entire construction of the Taj Mahal was completed.

From the number of years it took and the number of labourers who worked to complete the majestic Taj Mahal, you can clearly imagine how difficult it was to complete it at that time. But with continuous efforts and persistence, the labourers of that time proved that.

To achieve your grand success, you have to invest your time, you have to invest your hard work, you have to invest your caliber, and at the same time, you have to work with persistence, day and night until you accomplish your ultimate goal.

A scientist successfully invented his invention only because of his persistence.

A student would clear his examination only when he studies his lessons persistently.

The old fossils are formed into coal and petroleum due to persistent heat and pressure deep under the earth for millions of years.

A rich man wouldn't become a rich man only in a few days, a few months, or a few years, or merely by daydreaming or just by staying idle, doing nothing; he has to work persistently with his single-minded goal.

Behind every big success and grand glory of a man, there are tremendous efforts and persistence.

Persistence is the only key to your success.

Your persistence is the magical charm of your triumph.

With your persistence, you can turn anything in your favor.

With your persistence, you can do anything in your life.

With your persistence, you can turn the impossible into the possible.

With your persistence, you can achieve anything in your life.

It is your persistence that makes you a master in your work.

It is your persistence that makes you perfect in your work.

It is your persistence that makes you excellent in your work.

It is your persistence that makes you complete in your life.

Persistence wears out your weaknesses and negative energies from your mind, body, and soul.

It is not your good fortune that favors you, but the work of your persistence.

Let's take an example: take a light string and rub it on any hard surface or object, say, an iron bar or a hard rock, every day. After a few days, you'll notice some marks on the hard surface where you have rubbed persistently with the light string.

What does it tell you?

It tells you that with your persistent work, you can do impossible things in your life.

If you observe minutely around your surroundings, you'll always find many tiny creatures like ants, bees, butterflies, small birds, and many other living creatures. They are always working persistently on their daily needs without getting tired or retiring. They never give up. They do their best work persistently, no matter what happens.

If you see a small ant, then you'll see it is always moving for food; if you see a small bee, then you'll see it is always hovering over the blooming flowers for honey; if you see a small butterfly, then you'll see it is always fluttering its wings around the flowers for nectar; and if you see a small bird, then you'll see it is always flying hither and thither to feed itself.

Your persistent work is your true guide to moving ahead in your life. Whatever you want to achieve, whether it be name, fame, success, or glory, you have to work with persistence; only then will you accomplish great success in your life.

Your persistence never pushes you into the door of downfall,

But it will always hold you firmly.

It will always lead you to the door of great success.

Persistence is the natural order.

It is the fundamental law of our lives.

Without it, nobody could live in this world.

All the living creatures on this earth are bound by persistence.

Nobody could deny it or alter it.

We are all bound to work with persistence to live in this world.

Persistence is the only key to unlock your ceased fortune.

With persistence, you can achieve anything in your life.

Persistence is the only key to get your grand success.

Behind every big success and grand glory of a man, there is a tremendous persistence.

Think and Act

Persistence guarantees that results are inevitable.

> *---Paramahansa Yogananda*

Ambition is the path to success. Persistence is the vehicle you arrive in.

> *---Bill Bradley*

A river cuts through rock, not because of its power, but because of its persistence.

Persistence is to the character of man as carbon is to steel.

> *---Napolean Hill*

By persistence the snail reached the ark!

> *---C.H. Spurgeon*

---***---

5. *Focus*

Focus means concentration of all your six senses at one central point.

A farmer never grows his crops in his field if he is not focused on his farming.

A student never clears his exam if he is not focused on his studies.

A businessman never runs his business properly if he is not focused on his trade.

A scientist never invents new inventions if he is not focused on his experiments.

A sportsman never wins any championship or tournament in his life if he is not focused on his game.

A singer never sings well in his life if he is not focused on his singing.

A composer never composes hit songs in his life if he is not focused on his compositions.

An actor never plays a brilliant character in his life if he is not focused on his acting.

In every field, focus is the main criterion for success and growth.

Your focus is the guiding principle of your grand success.

Focus is your strength.

Focus is your energy.

Focus is your power.

Focus is your driving force.

Focus means your success.

If you focus on your life, you'll achieve whatever you want. Nothing is impossible for you to achieve in your life. Your success always demands complete focus from you. If you're focused on your goal, then nobody could ever dare to divert you from the path of your success. You'll reach your goal a hundred and one percent, and there is no doubt about it.

A focused person never diverts his mind; he will always concentrate on his goal. On the other hand, a person lacking focus will always divert his mind, and he will never achieve anything in his life.

A man never lives his life happily if he is not focused on his life. He will never do anything in his life. His life is like a fallen dry leaf that has no direction.

In every walk of life, you need your focus. You've got to focus on your life. You've got to focus on your world. You've got to focus on your family. You've got to focus on your relationships. You've got to focus on your work. Only then will you prosper in your life and live happily and peacefully.

If you're focused on your success, then you'll never have time to divert your mind anywhere. However, if you're not focused on your success, then you'll have enough time to divert your mind everywhere and anytime.

Focus makes you trained and disciplined in your life and gives you the right direction.

If you're focused, you'll definitely achieve success. If you're not focused, you'll surely witness failure. It is like the way you do your job and the way you accomplish tasks. Your focus always plays an important role in your success. Your focus is like your guide; it never allows you to move away from your destiny. It always leads you to the right path of success and halts you from the downfall of failure.

If you switch on the torchlight in any dark room, what will you see? You'll always see its light falling only in the center of the focused light without any diversion, and whatever is under it will be clearly visible.

Your focus is like the torchlight of your life. You've got to switch it on. In the darkness of failure, it's only your focus that will illuminate or mitigate your darkness and reveal the glorious brightness of your success.

Think for a second: if the rays of the sun are not focusing on our Earth and are diverting to some other planets, what will happen? There will be no existence of life on our Earth. Focus is a natural phenomenon. Everything is possible if you're focused on your life. It is your focus that assists you in moving ahead in your life. Your focus is the pathfinder of your success.

Focus is very significant for you if you want to achieve success in your life. Without total focus on your goal, there will be a hundred percent chance of diversion in your life, and you will never achieve anything.

Focus your mind, body, and soul only on your chosen goal. Forget the other insignificant things in your life. Go for it! Nobody will ever dare to obstruct you on the path to your success.

If you focus on good things, you'll always get good things. On the other hand, if you focus on bad things, you'll always get bad things. It is like you reap what you sow.

If you focus on your success, you'll always attain your success and satisfaction. If you don't focus on your success, you'll always face failure and disappointment.

Your focus is the driving force of your life. Your focus guarantees you your grand success. Therefore, it depends on you where you want to focus in your life.

If you're driving a car, a bike, or any other vehicle, what will you do while driving?

You'll always focus on the road ahead, holding the steering wheel of a car or the handle of a bike so that you can drive smoothly and control your vehicle.

On the contrary, what will happen if you're not focused on the road ahead? The moment you lose your focus on the road, you'll lose your balance, and you'll bump your car or bike against some other incoming vehicles. In the same fashion, if you're focused on the road of your life, then you can drive your vehicle of life smoothly and safely for many long distances, and ultimately you'll reach your chosen destiny. And if you're not focused on the road of your life, then you'll never reach anywhere, and you'll be lost in the middle of the crossroads.

Your focus is always directly proportional to your success.

When you're focused on your life, all your energy and power emerge from you, and you can do anything in your life. You'll gain tremendous strength and courage to do anything in your life. You'll become the storehouse of energy and power, and you'll excel and shine in your life.

When an earthquake occurs in any place, the maximum damage is always found at its epicenter, which means at the focus point. What does it tell us? It tells us that wherever the focus is greater, there is always maximum intensity of force and power. In a similar way, the more you focus on your aims and objectives, the more you perceive the chance to attain your grand success.

The sunlight burns a piece of paper when it is focused through a magnifying glass. What does it show you?

It shows you that if you keep your focus on anything, then it'll compel you to make it yours at any cost. Nobody will snatch it from you. You'll become its sole master eventually.

This shows you the power of focus.

There is tremendous power in your focus.

When you focus on your life, you'll become like the rays of the sun.

You can burn down every challenge in your life.

Your skills and talents will only grow and develop when you're focused on your life; otherwise, all your qualities are meaningless and worthless and will die prematurely.

It is only your focus that transforms your natural aptitudes into new forms and dimensions, prepares you, and leads you in the direction of excellence.

Many people fail in their lives even though they have equal skills and talents to any other successful people. But they fail.

Why?

It is only because they never focus on their lives. They allow their minds to roam like untamed animals.

Your life is like a camera. You've got to open the lens of your life and then give one hundred percent focus to it. Only then will you get a clear picture of your beautiful life and wonderful world.

If you want to focus on your life, then forget the other unnecessary things. Focus on your top priority. Focus on the main aims and objectives of your life. Never heed any other things. Then go for it. Don't try to divert your mind. You'll surely achieve your goal.

When a skillful archer sets his target, he only focuses on it. He always keeps his mind and body steady and maintains his nerves cool and calm. He controls everything utterly. He even holds his breath for a moment in order to focus his eyes on his target. When everything is set in the right place and he assures himself, he finally releases the arrow from his bow toward the target. His shooting arrow never misses its mark; it hits straight on the bull's eye.

Be like a skillful archer in your life.

Set your target and focus on it.

You'll never miss the target of your life.

Decide on your own field where you want to focus in your life, and then give your mind, heart, and soul wholeheartedly. And go for it. Give your hundred and one percent effort. Success will always be yours.

If you're focused on your goals in life, you'll see your grand success and glory even from a distance, and even in the darkness of your life. You'll never become disheartened in your life. You'll get clear glimpses of your triumph and attain it no matter what happens.

Always remember that if you're not focused on your life, then you'll always wander aimlessly and live your life like a nomad. Your focus is one of the key factors in your grand success. Your focus opens your closed mind. Your focus awakens your dizzy heart. Your focus salvages your soul. Your focus gives you new directions in your life. Your focus enlightens your dark world.

If you want grand success in your life, then focus on your chosen goal. Never divert your mind, heart, and soul. Only focus on your aims and objectives. You'll always witness your bright success and glory.

Only focus on your goals. Only focus on your life. Only focus on your world. Your success is always determined by your focus.

Your focus is the torch light of your life.

Your focus is one of the key factors of your grand success.

Think and Act

Focus on where you want to be, not where you were, or where you are.

Focus on your goal. Don't look in any direction but ahead.

Stop getting distracted by things that have nothing to do with your goals.

Focus on the present and the past will take care of itself.

Concentrate all your thoughts upon the work at hand. The sun's rays do not burn until brought to a focus.

---Alexander Graham Bell

F.......Follow

O......One

C.......Course

U.......Until

S........Successful

---***---

6. Failure

Failure is a part of your life. If there is life, there is failure too. If there is life, there is success too. You can never deny it, and nobody could ever deny it either. Success and failure are like the two sides of the same coin; where there is success, there is failure too. It is like a package deal. We can say it is like day and night.

Enjoy your failure like you enjoy your success. Welcome it with an open mind and heart. Treat it as your teacher. Learn from it. Improve yourself. But never allow it to rule you. Tame it like your galloping horse, and march ahead on the road to your success.

It is very important to face failure in your life before you taste the sweetness of your grand success. It will give you more happiness and contentment. However, if you get the sweet taste of success in the very first instance, then you might not face the bitter encounter of failure later on.

If you face failure in your initial attempt, then you'll get enough time to adjust and acclimatize yourself, and you too will be able to cope with every harsh situation of your failure. You could prepare yourself right from the very beginning; you could transform yourself from good to better, and from better to best. You'll become a master of your chosen goals. You'll be able to judge your strong points and weak points. You'll know everything about yourself. You could awaken your hidden skills and talents. You could examine yourself thoroughly. You'll become more cautious. You'll become more confident. You'll gain more self-esteem. You'll become more disciplined. You'll become more responsible. You'll grow and mature. You'll become stronger than you were in your previous attempts. You'll become more courageous and valiant than you were in the past. You'll make a new plan with different moves and strategies to face the next level of your challenges.

The best part of your failure is learning new lessons and gaining new experiences from it, which will help you improve further.

If you fear failure, you'll never do anything right in your life. You'll never learn anything, and you'll always remain behind everybody and everything.

If you fear failure, it means you fear trying something new. And when you never try to do new things in your life, you'll never achieve anything; you'll never change your life; you'll never bring differences into your life; and you'll never know the beauties of your life and the thrilling mysteries of this world.

Learn to accept your failures as your victories.

Take it as your learning experience.

Take it as your new challenge.

Take it as your new way.

Take it as your new approach.

Take it as your new turning point.

Take it as your new opportunity.

Take it as your new transformation.

But never give up trying.

When Thomas Alva Edison failed many times in his experiments, one of his friends asked him, "You failed so many times; why don't you stop your experiments?"

In reply, Thomas Alva Edison said, "I found a thousand new ways in my every failure." All the great legends in the history of mankind are great failures in their respective fields in their initial endeavors; but they never gave up. They kept trying while learning new lessons and gaining experience from their bitter failures.

Learn good lessons from your failures.

Gain knowledge from your failures.

Earn experience from your failures.

Find new ideas from your failures.

Discover new solutions from your failures.

When a small child takes its first step on the ground, it falls down countless times. It tries to sit on its back; then it tries to get up by itself; it tries to crawl; it tries to stand up; and finally, it tries to walk. In every moment of its initial steps, a small child falls down many times, but at the same time, it learns the lessons of how to walk properly. It never gives up until it learns to walk and run properly.

I still remembered very clearly the days when I started to learn to ride a bicycle for the first time. I had fallen down many times and got bruises on my face, injured my hands, elbows, knees, and legs. But every time I fell, I learned new lessons and new techniques about riding a bicycle, and I tried to improve myself every day. Many onlookers laughed at me when I fell on the road. Even some of them advised me to stop riding a bicycle. However, I didn't quit learning to ride my bicycle because I knew that I could ride like my other friends. I corrected every shortcoming in my bicycle riding, and after a couple of months, I learned to ride my bicycle like an expert cyclist. And then what? Every morning and evening, I went out on my bicycle while talking with the whizzing wind.

When you fail in your life while doing something new, never take it seriously. Take it easy and lightly. Thank Almighty God that you get another golden opportunity to do something great. Initiate your work with a fresh mind. Set up your work with innovative ideas. Take full advantage of it, and go for it with full preparation and enthusiasm. You'll surely find your success on the way, waiting for you with a grin.

"I've missed more than 9,000 shots in my career. I've lost almost 300 games. 26 times I've been trusted to take the game-winning shot and missed. I've failed over and over and over again in my life, and that is why I succeed."

---Michael Jordan

If you want to learn the great lessons of life, then never run away from your failures. Face your failures like a brave soldier. Always keep in your mind that until you accept your failure, you will never witness success in your life, and nobody could ever dare to force you. It is only you who would choose failure as your stepping stone to success or a falling step to downfall. It depends on you how you perceive or react to your failure.

We all learn everything while falling down and facing bitter failure in our lives. This is the law of this world. You have to accept it.

When a potter rolls the wheel to make a pot, he does not make a perfect pot on his first attempt. It takes him many long days and months to become a perfect potter.

You are like a potter in your life. You have to give some time to yourself in order to become perfect and skillful in your areas of endeavor.

Albert Einstein

His teachers called him "slow" and "mentally handicapped." He also didn't speak until he turned 4 and didn't read until he was 7.

Amitabh Bachchan

He was rejected for a job at All India Radio because of his heavy voice.

Abdul Kalam

He was rejected in the interview for a pilot position.

Sachin Tendulkar

He failed in the 8th standard.

Lionel Messi

He used to serve tea at a shop to support his football training.

J.K. Rowling

Her book 'Harry Potter' was rejected 12 times by publishers.

Bill Gates

He didn't even complete his university education. Today, he is the richest man in the world and the founder of Microsoft.

Sylvester Stallone

He was rejected 1,500 times when selling his script and himself for the famous Rocky film.

Colonel Sanders

He was turned down 1,009 times when he was selling his chicken recipe at the ripe age of 65. He founded KFC.

Thomas Alva Edison

He found 10,000 ways not to create a light bulb before succeeding.

They all faced and witnessed the bitter taste of failure, but they never gave up; they accepted their failures as the stepping stones to their success. They knew very well that their failures were the pillars of their great success.

Once upon a time, a defeated king named Robert Bruce, who had lost all his battles and his kingdom, escaped for his life and wandered hither and thither, hiding himself inside a cave in the jungle. He was very sad and deserted, having lost all hope, spending his days and nights in despair for many days.

Then one fine day, when he was lost in his wandering thoughts, he saw a tiny spider that was trying to knit its web from one end of the cave wall to the other. The tiny spider failed every time it tried to knit its web, but it didn't give up. It tried again and again, even after failing countless times. Finally, after many tiresome failures, it successfully knitted its web to the other end of the cave wall.

King Robert Bruce was enlightened while witnessing the grit of the tiny spider. He took a lesson from it and then resumed his fresh attempts to conquer his lost kingdom and glory.

In the end, he too won back whatever he had lost.

Try to perceive your success in every failure. Accept your failures with an open heart and open arms; hug them like your best buddy, and then learn the hidden lessons and messages from them. Try to overcome your shortcomings and negativities. You'll definitely achieve your grand success in the end.

Abraham Lincoln's Famous Failures:

1832: He lost a job.

1832: He was defeated for the legislature.

1833: He failed in business.

1834: He was elected to the legislature.

1835: His sweetheart (Ann Rutledge) died.

1836: He had a nervous breakdown.

1838: He was defeated for speaker.

1843: He was defeated for the nomination for Congress.

1846: He was elected to Congress.

1848: He lost re-nomination.

1849: He was rejected for Land Officer.

1854: He was defeated for the Senate.

1856: He was defeated for the nomination for Vice-President.

1858: He was again defeated for the Senate.

1860: He was elected President of the United States of America.

Always remember that your failure is temporary, and so is your success. It will never be permanent. But, yes, it is up to you how you can convert your failure into your glorious victory.

Your failure is very significant for your learning lessons and gaining experience in your life.

Your lessons and experiences always count in your life.

Your failure is the first stepping stone to your success. Accept it gladly with an open mind, heart, and soul. Your glorious success is always waiting for you.

Behind every light, there is a dark shadow, and behind every dark shadow, there is a golden dazzling light. Likewise, behind every failure of yours, there is a shining light of your grand success.

Failure is only a momentary,

It's temporary.

No doubt, it bends your road,

But it can't block your road.

Even success is not permanent,

You need your temperament.

Your hope is your golden ray,

Showing you your hidden way.

Don't cry,

Never say die.

Believe in yourself,

Work on yourself.

Try to get up!

Try to rise up!

Don't make your heart weak,

Make your heart strong.

When you turn your failure into success,

Then you'll definitely achieve your sparkling success.

Never mind failure,

Your failure is the stepping stone

That leads you to the ultimate milestone.

Your failure is the first stepping stone of your success.

Behind every failure of yours, there is a shining light of your grand success.

Think and Act

We learn from failure not from success.

Failure doesn't mean the game is over, it means try again with experience.

---Len Schlesinger

Success is not final, failure is not fatal: it is the courage to continue that counts.

---Winston Churchill

Failure is simply the opportunity to begin again, this time more intelligently.

---Henry Ford

The only failure is when you say, "I give up!"

---***---

7. Positivity

If you want to gear up your vehicle of life to the door of success without any breaks or blockages, then you must be positive in every move and every approach.

Positivity is very important for your growth and development in life. No positivity, no growth, and no development in your life. Positivity means the dwelling of positive energy in your life. Negativity means the dwelling of negative energy in your life.

Without positivity in your thoughts, ideas, plans, decisions, and actions, you won't move ahead in your life. Positivity is the only vital force that will control your life. Without it, your life is impossible. Without it, you'll become directionless. Your life will become sick and mediocre.

Positivity means you're optimistic in your life.

Positivity means you're constructive in your life.

Positivity means you're courageous in your life.

Positivity means you're confident in your life.

Positivity means you're active in your life.

Positivity means you're motivated in your life.

Positivity means you're certain in your life.

Positive means you're definite in your life.

Positive means you're sure in your life.

Positive means you're clear in your life.

Positive means you love yourself.

Positive means you love your family.

Positive means you love your friend.

Positive means you love your work.

Always remember, no positive, no life.

No life, no world.

When you're positive in your life, you can view your destiny from a distance. You'll see everything with your clear vision. Nothing will remain hidden from you. What others won't perceive, you would visualize everything, crystal clear. You would discover or invent what others couldn't think or imagine, even in their wildest dreams. You could easily comprehend everything for yourself. You don't need to go anywhere. You would obtain everything at your doorstep.

If you want wonders in your life,

Then always think positively and act positively.

If you want miracles in your life,

Then always think positively and act positively.

If you want everlasting happiness and peace in your life,

Then always think positively and act positively.

If you want to become a winner in your life,

Then always think positively and act positively.

If you want grand success in your life,

Then always think positively and act positively.

There is great power in positivity. When you have positivity in your thoughts and in your actions, you can achieve anything in your life. Nothing is impossible for you.

We all are surviving in this world only because of our positive thoughts, positive ideas, positive plans, positive decisions, and positive actions.

Your positive outlook makes a great difference in your life.

One day in Singapore, a woman of fifty years went to the doctor to check her breathing problem in the hospital. The doctor diagnosed her and declared in a sad tone, "Madam, I am very sorry. You have heart cancer in the last stage."

The woman smiled and said, "How long will I survive?"

The doctor hesitated and said, "Madam, I am afraid you wouldn't survive more than six months."

"Oh, thank God!" the woman heaved a sigh of relief and said with a grin, "At least I have got six months to enjoy my life."

She paid the fee to the doctor and left the hospital in a hurry.

The doctor was dumbfounded by an unexpected response from the woman. After six months, the woman met the same doctor once again for a check-up. When the doctor re-examined the woman, he was astonished to find that the woman who was in the last stage of heart cancer six months ago was perfectly all right; there was no sign of any cancer. "Madam," the doctor said with an implausible tone, "it is a miracle... It is a miracle... Madam, you're perfectly all right." "Thank you, doctor," the woman said with a contented smile. Later, the doctor asked the woman how she had performed that miracle on herself.

The woman narrated that she was positive about her life. She started loving herself more than she had ever loved herself before. She knew that she would survive even though she was suffering from that terrible disease. She woke up early in the morning in a happy mood, with new hope and new positive thoughts every day. She started singing her favorite songs; she started watching her favorite movies; she started playing her favorite games and sports; she started doing meditation, yoga, and physical exercise; she started engaging herself in social activities; she hung out in her favorite places with her close friends and relatives; she started living her life to the fullest; and she enjoyed every moment with fun and feasting. And then eventually that miracle happened to her.

Your positive thoughts do miracles in your life.

One day, a man landed in a place of dry, sandy, and rocky land, and he dreamed of changing that desert-like place into a beautiful and evergreen forest. When he related his dream to his wife, his family members, and his close friends and associates, they all said that it was impossible to turn that wasteland into anything worthwhile.

However, he was firm in his dream. He was positive in his outlook and approach. He was determined to execute that impossible task. So, from the very next day, he started collecting the seeds of plants and trees that suited that desert-like land and began working He worked half a day for his dream project apart from his regular work every day. After twenty-five years, he accomplished his dream and turned it into an amazing reality. He transformed that desert-like land into a beautiful and evergreen forest. He turned his dream into reality with his positive thoughts, positive actions, and positive self-belief.

Your positive thoughts can transform you.

You can do anything in your life.

Nothing is impossible in your life if you have positive thoughts, positive actions, and positive self-belief.

In a small town, two brothers grew up together. Their father was one of the most wanted thieves in the town, and one day he was shot dead by the police in an encounter. They had lost their mother when they were merely of tender age. The elder brother worked very hard; he became an honest man and earned his living with a good profession. On the other hand, the younger brother became the same most wanted thief in the town as his father on his dream project.

The elder brother viewed the positive sides of his life and earned a decent living; on the contrary, the younger brother focused on the negative aspects of his life, lived an illicit life, and now and then tried to escape from the law. One day, he was shot dead by the police in an encounter, meeting the same fate as his father.

If you view the positive sides of your life,

you'll always rise up in your life.

If you view the negative sides of your life,

you'll always fall down in your life.

You'll become the way you view your life.

When the great explorer Christopher Columbus set out on his voyage in the Atlantic Ocean from Spain with the hope of finding new lands and great treasures, he did not think that he would discover the Americas in his journey in the year 1492. However, he discovered America by accident, and his name was remembered forever as the great explorer.

However, his voyage was not an easy and smooth one; he had to counter numerous hurdles and upheavals. He lost many of his comrades and crew members on his voyage. Even on one occasion, his own crew members tried to kill him for not halting the journey midway. But he was positive in his approach. He knew that he would find something worthwhile at the end of his journey.

Columbus won the confidence of his crew members with his positive approach and insights, and eventually, he proved successful.

Always keep your positive thoughts within you.

It'll change your mind.

Always keep your positive emotions within you.

It'll change your heart.

Always keep your positive ideas within you.

It'll change your life.

Always keep your positive principles within you.

It'll change your lifestyle.

Always keep your positive attitudes within you.

It'll change your personality.

Always keep your positive energy within you.

It'll change your world.

If you're positive, you'll never become dawdling in your life.

Never be negative in your life, no matter what happens. Always be positive in your life.

Motivation comes to you when you're positive.

Inspiration comes to you when you're positive.

Self-belief comes to you when you're positive.

Self-confidence comes to you when you're positive.

Deprivation comes to you when you're negative.

Disgrace comes to you when you're negative.

Self-doubt comes to you when you're negative.

Insecurity comes to you when you're negative.

A positive man says, 'Let us find out;' a negative man says, "Nobody knows."

When a positive man makes a mistake, he says, 'I was wrong;' when a negative man makes mistakes, he says, "It was not my fault.'

A positive man goes through a problem; a negative man goes around it and never gets past it.

A positive man makes commitments; a negative man makes promises.

A positive man says, 'I am good, but not as good as I ought to be;' a negative man says, 'I am not as bad as a lot of other people.'

A positive man tries to learn from those who are superior to him; a negative man tries to tear down those who are superior to him.

A positive man says, 'There ought to be a better way to do it;' a negative man says, 'That is the way it is always done here.'

If you want a good life,

then always be positive, whatever happens in your life.

If you want a happy life,

then always be positive, whatever happens in your life.

If you want a peaceful life,

then always be positive, whatever happens in your life.

If you want a successful life,

then always be positive, whatever happens in your life.

If you want a dignified life,

then always be positive, whatever happens in your life.

If you want a glorious life,

then always be positive, whatever happens in your life.

Be always positive.

There is a great energy and power in your positivity.

When you're positive, then nothing is impossible for you.

Think and Act

Think like a proton and stay positive.

The positive thinker sees the invisible, feels the intangible, and achieves the impossible.

---Winston Churchill

Once you replace negative thoughts with positive ones, you'll start having positive results.

---Willie Nelson

You can't live a positive life with a negative mind.

Train your mind to see the positive in every situation.

---***---

8. You must believe your abilities

You're born with your natural abilities. There is nobody in this world who is born without natural abilities. Everybody is born with his or her natural abilities. But it is very unfortunate that many of them fail to discover their natural abilities and spend their entire lives in mediocrity and wandering.

What are my natural abilities?

Have you ever asked this question of yourself?

If not, then ask yourself now.

Ask this question of yourself until you know your natural abilities.

Once you know your natural abilities, you'll know how to proceed in your life, and you'll know what to do in your life. You'll know the actual mission of your life. You'll know the ways to your success. You'll know the real purpose of your existence in this world.

You're born with a brain to think.

You're born with two eyes to see.

You're born with one nose to smell.

You're born with one mouth to speak.

You're born with one tongue to taste.

You're born with two hands to work.

You're born with two legs to walk.

To think, to see, to speak, to smell, to taste, to work, and to walk—these are all your natural abilities, which you've inherited right from your birth.

You never deny that you can think with your brain; you never deny that you can see with your two eyes; you never deny that you can smell with your nose; you never deny that you can speak with your mouth; you never deny that you can taste with your tongue; you never deny that you can work with your two hands; and you never deny that you can walk with your two legs.

However, if you're ever denied all your natural abilities, then you're not only bringing shame on yourself and your parents, but you're also disgracing Almighty God, who has bestowed upon you your natural abilities to live a meaningful and purposeful life in this world.

You can think because you believe in the abilities of your brain.

You can see because you believe in the abilities of your two eyes.

You can smell because you believe in the abilities of your nose.

You can speak because you believe in the abilities of your mouth.

You can taste because you believe in the abilities of your tongue.

You can work because you believe in the abilities of your two hands.

You can walk because you believe in the abilities of your two legs.

But the moment you stop believing in your abilities, you'll lose every bit of your self-confidence, self-belief, and self-esteem. Then your downfall and downgrading will start the very moment in your life.

It is the universal truth that everybody is born with natural abilities.

If you can think well, then believe it; this is your natural ability.

If you can imagine well, then believe it; this is your natural ability.

If you can plan well, then believe it; this is your natural ability.

If you can make good decisions, then believe it; this is your natural ability.

If you can judge well, then believe it; this is your natural ability.

If you can manage well, then believe it; this is your natural ability.

If you can talk well, then believe it; this is your natural ability.

If you can read well, then believe it; this is your natural ability.

If you can remember well, then believe it; this is your natural ability.

If you can teach well, then believe it; this is your natural ability.

If you can observe well, then believe it; this is your natural ability.

If you can learn well, then believe it; this is your natural ability.

If you can write well, then believe it; this is your natural ability.

If you can paint well, then believe it; this is your natural ability.

If you can compose well, then believe it; this is your natural ability.

If you can sing well, then believe it; this is your natural ability.

If you can dance well, then believe it; this is your natural ability.

If you can play well, then believe it; this is your natural ability.

If you can act well, then believe it; this is your natural ability.

If you can run well, then believe it; this is your natural ability.

If you can work hard, then believe it; this is your natural ability.

It is the law of nature that every creature inherits some special ability to survive in this world.

A bird can fly in the sky.

An animal can run very fast.

A reptile can crawl on the land.

A fish can swim in the water.

You too have special abilities to make your life amazing and grand.

Your abilities are the ingredients and catalysts of your success.

Your abilities are your boons.

Always believe it, no matter what happens in your life.

If you have abilities, then you have nothing to worry about.

Your abilities will lead you toward your goal.

A farmer couldn't yield good crops until he could believe in his farming abilities.

A student couldn't pass his examination until he could believe in his ability to remember his lessons.

A player couldn't win any match until he could believe in his playing abilities.

An actor couldn't act brilliantly until he could believe in his acting abilities.

A dancer couldn't dance gracefully until he could believe in his dancing abilities.

A singer couldn't sing well until he could believe in his singing abilities.

A writer couldn't write well until he could believe in his writing abilities.

A businessman couldn't run his business successfully until he could believe in his business abilities.

A soldier couldn't defeat his enemies until he could believe in his warfare abilities.

A scientist couldn't invent new inventions until he could believe in his researching abilities.

A mountaineer couldn't scale the highest peak until he could believe in his mountaineering abilities.

A winner couldn't win until he could believe in his winning abilities.

You couldn't succeed in your life until you could believe in your abilities.

If you believe in your natural abilities, you can do anything in your life.

You'll find a way wherever you put your footsteps.

In the Paralympic Games, all the participants are either disabled or physically unsound, but the manner in which they display their abilities in sports is highly commendable. They play with high spirit and zest like normal sportsmen. And they win gold medals for their respective countries. All of this is only possible because they believe in their winning abilities.

Always believe in your natural abilities. If you ever stop believing in your abilities, the very moment you do, you will become disabled or handicapped, and you'll commit a crime against yourself.

You're born with your natural abilities to be a winner and to be successful in your life. You have every right to make yourself the best and perfect in your life. And nobody could ever dare to hinder you from enhancing your abilities. You've inherited your natural abilities to make yourself worthy and successful in your life.

Believe in your abilities.

Your abilities never betray you.

It is only your abilities that lead you to your ultimate goal.

Your abilities are the source of your success.

If you believe in your abilities, you'll do anything in your life. Your success depends on your abilities. If you have ability, you have success. But if you lack ability, you only have failure.

Your ability always guarantees you grand success.

Believe in your abilities. It'll change your entire life and your whole world. It is only your ability that will transform you completely.

Believe in your abilities. It can move away every Himalayan-like task. Believe in your abilities. It is the only key to unlock your sealed door of success.

You're born with tremendous natural abilities. Search within you. Nourish it every day. Exploit it every moment. Your abilities are your energy and power. It is only your abilities that will make everything possible. Always believe in your abilities.

Your abilities are the ingredients and catalysts of your success.

Always believe in your abilities.

Think and Act

Ability is what gives you the opportunity; belief is what gets you there.

---Apollo

Do not lower your goals to the height of your abilities. Instead, heighten your abilities to the level of your goals.

Always trust in your own abilities. Even when you think you can't......You can.

One of the best ways to give yourself meaning in life is to continue to challenge your abilities.

---Donald Lynn Frost

Nothing can challenge your ability, even difficulties cannot!!

---Kelvin

---***---

9. Self-help

Self-help is the best help. Nobody can help you better than you yourself because you know yourself better than anyone else. Nobody will help you. It's only you who helps you every moment of your life.

Self-help means you're relying on yourself.

Self-help means you're growing yourself.

Self-help means you're developing yourself.

Self-help means you're enriching your life.

Self-help means you're rising up.

Self-help means you're building your strength.

Self-help means you're building your self-belief.

Self-help means you're making yourself self-reliant.

Self-help means you're making yourself self-confident.

Self-help means you're making yourself disciplined.

In the juncture of your life, when you tumble down in the middle of the crossroads, you'll never find anyone to hold your falling and trembling hands. At that very moment, you will have to get up yourself while helping yourself.

A small crawling child couldn't walk properly until it tried to help itself. In a similar way, you're like a small crawling child in every walk of life. You've got to try to help yourself.

If you want to walk properly on the road of your life, then you've got to help yourself. If you want to run smoothly on the road of your life, then you've got to help yourself.

You're your own best friend if you help yourself. You're your own worst foe if you do not help yourself.

No doubt, sometimes you might find someone who is willing to hold your first step, but only for a time, because you've got to take your own next step. When a person falls sick, it depends on him whether he visits the doctor or not. And if he visits the doctor, then it is also up to him whether he takes the medicine prescribed by the doctor or not. The point here is whether he helps himself or not.

In the journey of life, at some point in time, you'll always find yourself surrounded by hardships and troubles, but it is up to you how you deal with them—whether you face them bravely or flee cowardly. If you're facing your hardships and troubles bravely, then you're helping yourself. But if you're running away from your hardships and troubles, then you're misleading yourself and inviting more hardships and troubles into your life.

You can only solve your problems in life by helping yourself. But you can't solve your problems in life if you're running away from them.

Once upon a time, a saintly man was living in a small village. He was a devoted and God-fearing man. Everyone revered him for his ease and virtuous life. One day, a very heavy flood occurred in the village. All the villagers left the village before the floodwaters rushed into their houses.

However, the saintly man was very composed and carefree. Instead of leaving his house, he started praying to God. The village folks asked him to leave his house as soon as possible and join them in a safe place. But he refused to accompany them.

When the floodwaters reached the ground floor of his house, a boat came to take him. But he denied it. He said that God would come to save him.

Then, when the floodwaters reached the roof of his house, a big ship came to take him. But once again, he denied it. He said that God would come to save him.

Finally, when he was about to drown in the floodwaters, a helicopter came to rescue him, but he denied it. He said that God would come to save him. And he drowned and died.

When the man reached heaven after his death, he complained to God about why He didn't save him when he was drowned in the floodwaters. At his complaint, God smiled and said, "My dear child, I have come to you three times to save your life, but you denied yourself the opportunity to accompany me on all three occasions."

When the poor man heard God's reply, he bowed down his head in disgrace and realized his own errors.

Always remember that God helps those who help themselves.

If you want happiness, prosperity, success, and glory in your life, then you must help yourself. You will never achieve anything merely by wishing and daydreaming in your life. In order to achieve something in your life, you must act practically and help yourself.

A caterpillar couldn't transform itself into a beautiful butterfly if it didn't try to help itself come out of the sealed cocoon. Many people couldn't make a great mark in their lives because they never try to help themselves break free from the barriers of worldly cocoons and spend their entire lives in doom.

The moment you stop helping yourself, you'll lose your own credentials in life. And the moment you start helping yourself, you'll regain your own credentials in life.

Nobody will help you when you tumble down into a deep ditch. It is only you who can lift yourself up. Never wait for anybody. Make yourself your own helping hand. Only you can help yourself best. Even Almighty God helps those who help themselves. Help yourself. Believe in yourself. Self-help is the best help.

Self-help is the best help.

The moment you stop helping yourself, you'll lose your own credentials of your life.

Think and Act

If no one is there to push you, drag yourself. You cannot always depend on others to help you out; you also have to help yourself.

All the advice in the world will never help you until you help yourself.

---Fred Van Amburgh

A person has two hands, one for helping himself, the other for helping others.

To help yourself, you must be yourself. Be the best that you can be. When you make a mistake, learn from it. Pick yourself up and move on.

75

The best place to find a helping hand is at the end of your own arm.

---Swedish Proverb

---***---

10. Success is a journey

A journey of a thousand miles begins with a small step.

You never reach anywhere the moment you start your journey. It takes some time to reach your destination. But every small step you take will count in your journey. You never reach anywhere in one single jump. You have to walk step by step, slowly and steadily, continuously and tirelessly. Only then will you reach where you want to go.

You never build a house in a day.

You never build your career in a day.

You never become a perfect man in a day.

You never become a successful man in a day.

You never become a wealthy man in a day.

It will always take some days, some weeks, some months, and some years.

It will always require your hard work, dedication, enthusiasm, and patience.

You will have to go on and on, slowly and steadily, putting every small step in the right direction.

You never build the foundation of your life in a day or in a hurry. Every moment, you need your small steps. The journey of a river always begins with a source of small spring water under the earth. Then, it starts its flowing journey slowly and continuously through the ocean.

If you want to examine yourself, then open a tap and let the water fall in small drops into an empty bucket. Check your time. After some time, say after half an hour or after one hour, you'll find the empty bucket full of water. What does it show? It shows that every small drop of water counts to fill an empty bucket.

In a similar way, if you want to fill the empty bucket of your life, then you have to allow every small drop of your energy and power in a constructive manner. Then you'll see the empty bucket of your life fill with happiness and prosperity.

In every business venture, every small gain or profit will count towards the progress and growth of a business. No business will progress and grow overnight, in a day, in a week, in a month, or in a year. It will take many years to reach the level of a successful business house.

If you want to save some money in your bank account, what would you plan initially? Obviously, you would plan to save a small amount of money from your monthly earnings so that you can spend your money in the near future for a good cause.

For instance, if you save a minimum of 500 rupees every month as your small saving amount, then after twenty-five years, you will manage to save 150,000 rupees in your account. This means that in your savings account, every small amount of money that you save each month will count towards making a big amount of money.

It is the same case in everything you deal with in your life. Whatever you do in your life, whether you do a small amount of work or a large amount of work, everything you do will count at the end of the day.

Your life is like a simple addition.

See the simple additions given below and analyze yourself.

1 + 1 + 1 + 1 + 1 + 1 + 1 + 1 + 1 + 1 = 10

10 + 10 + 10 + 10 + 10 + 10 + 10 + 10 + 10 + 10 = 100

100 + 100 + 100 + 100 + 100 + 100 + 100 + 100 + 100 + 100 = 1000

1000 + ... = 10,000

10,000 + ... = 100,000

....
....

And so on.....

Have you ever seen a small plant grow fully into a big tree overnight?

No. You never see such a plant. It is never possible.

A small seed turns into a seedling in two to three days, then a seedling turns into a small plant in a week, and a small plant turns into a big tree after many days, many months, and many years.

You're like a small plant. You'll grow gradually, day after day, night after night, week after week, month after month, and year after year. Then, one day, you'll become like a big tree after many years.

If you ever read the life stories of great men and women, then you'll know how they started their early lives with every small step.

They always greeted every small step as the greatest step of their success. For them, every small step was as important as their lives. They knew how to turn their small steps into big steps. That's why they created legacies in their lives, became great men and women, and inspired every generation of mankind.

In the Olympic Games, many world records have been broken by numerous sportsmen and sportswomen, but behind their records, there are countless small steps.

They all faced many odds and challenges in their lives. They practiced very hard and prepared themselves for many days, weeks, months, and years for the Olympic Games, forgetting and sacrificing every bit of their comfort and leisure, utilizing every drop of their energy and power.

Every small step you take today will lead you toward the ladder of your great success and glory.

Your success always depends on every small step that you take, not on the big steps you jump. Every small step is significant for you because it is the key to your great success and glory.

Never worry about your small steps. Keep your small steps firm, whether it is like a tortoise's walk or a snail's pace. Keep your small steps continuous and tireless. You'll definitely reach your goal in the end.

But only worry when you try to take big steps. Many people try to jump into big steps and collapse at the very first step on their road to success.

Behind every big success, there are countless small steps of failure.

Take your every small step

One by one

Step by step

Every day and every night

But never be afraid of your small steps.

Every small step you take will make a huge difference in your
life.

Just keep continuing your small steps.

Never forget that you too grow every day and every night

Slowly and slowly.

Step by step.

Nothing will grow or develop overnight.

It is the law of nature.

Every small step you take will count in your growth and
development.

Your success is not in taking big steps,

but in converting every small step into a big result.

***Your success always depends on your every small step that
you take. But not the big steps you jump into.***

Think and Act

Take small steps each day. You might not get there today, but you'll be closer than yesterday.

Success is not a big step in the future, success is a small step taken right now.

Sometimes the smallest step in the right direction ends up being the biggest step on your life. Tip toe if you must, but take the step.

Even when it's hard to move, take small steps forward. Because every step will lead you farther away from where you were yesterday.

It is better to take many small steps in the right direction than to make a great leap forward only to stumble backward.

---Old Chinese Proverb

---***---

About the author:

Birister Sharma is a full time author. He is also an avid reader. He loves reading, writing, and motivation. He has penned down dozens of self-help motivational books and novels so far.

You may contact him @ birister2007@gmail.com